Row in the Unknown

A poetry anthology where Row finds themselves

Rowan O'Keefe

Row in the Unknown by Rowan O'Keefe

Published by Rowan O'Keefe
http://www.rowintheunknown.wordpress.com

Copyright © 2022 Rowan O'Keefe
ISBN: 9798849002644

To Robert and Ann.
The three musketeers

ALL proceeds from sales of 'Row in the Unknown' will be donated to 'Spectra London'.

CONTENTS

It is recommended that this anthology is read by those who are either adults or 'older teens' who are able to cope with the topics mentioned on this page.

There are trigger/content warnings for the following topics in this anthology:

- Sibling birth
- Autistic Spectrum Condition – understanding
- Suicidal ideation
- Term 'abuse' mentioned
- Involuntary referral to CAMHS (Child and Adolescent Mental Health Services)
- Eating disorders
- Inpatient psychiatric hospital admission
- Being involuntarily sectioned in a psychiatric ward
- Self-harm ideation
- Suicidal ideation
- Being isolated in a contained space involuntarily
- Loss of friends
- Family issues
- Abandonment difficulties
- Mental health difficulties mentioned throughout

ROW IN THE UNKNOWN

Nursery

Boys on the left.
Girls on the right.
But where does little Aoife sit?

She just sees it in 'black and white'.

Little Aoife did not feel

As though she 'fit' on either side.

But there are rules, explains her teacher,
And she knows that, when there are rules, she must abide.

But instead of sitting with the 'girls'

Who are 'lovely and friendly and like me';
She sits directly in the middle
So that they cannot define her in a binary.

Little Aoife failed to understand
That this would be a beginning of a journey.
A adventure to self-discovery
Where there would be ups, downs, twisting, curving.

But Little Aoife did know
That she did not want to be a female.
She also did not know that she did not need to be;
She could fit into wherever she wanted on the gender scale.

It will take twenty years for you to learn this, Aoife,
But I promise, with all my heart, it will be worth it.

Just because you don't 'fit in' now,

Does not mean that you can't eventually conquer it.

Play

I am in Nanny's garden, surrounded by toys.

'Go on, then, Aoife, why don't you have a play?'
I struggle with this idea, this concept;
What am I supposed to do or say?

I stare at the toys. Thomas the Tank Engine.
My favourite show to watch on TV.
But how do I make my own story with these 'objects'?
How do I make this about me?

I look at my Cabbage Patch doll, 'Ruby',
And gently stroke her hair.
Is this what Nanny means by 'playing'?

Because I am bored and confused; it's not fair.

Nanny is busying herself in the garden,
Pulling out old flowers and weeds.
She spots me in the corner of her eye
And looks as though she could weep.

Instead, Nanny offers that I use the hose
And, to water the flowers, the watering can.
This is an instruction, something I can do
And I feel it is set as a challenge.

I try my best, and I'm smiling;
I am helping, following rules, a reason.
In my denim, pinafore dress, feeling a purpose.

To what I am doing, which isn't pointlessly 'playing'.

Nanny says I can garden with her whenever I want
Which fills me with complete and utter joy.
But she also shows me how to play with Thomas and Ruby,
With what is equally important for a three-year-old: toys.

Brother's Birth

Mummy, Daddy, Aoife,
The way it has been since day one.
But now you are here, a part of the family

And I cannot help but feel overcome.

Visiting you at the hospital
Was heartbreaking but so vital
For me to realise that it was no longer just three;
It is now four. I remember my exact recital:

'He's so little. Look at his hands, and his feet!'
I could not get over how adorable you were.
But crushing my insides, choking my throat
Was the feeling that you were stealing him and her.

Him and her, Mummy and Daddy,
However you want to refer to them.
They are not mine; they are ours.

And I don't know how, from him, to deter them.

I am so lucky to have you in my life, but saying that
I struggle with you taking away a part of me.
A part that felt that I was involved in family life,
Which, although I still am, it feels as though it has departed me.

I love you, brother, and I always will,
I just am getting my thoughts down on paper.
You are simultaneously the best and worst thing

That ever happened to me. And I guess that's hard to decipher.

Not Verbally Verbal

My brother has a way of communicating
That is not always with words.
But, like me, when he is sad he cries
And when he is happy? Hilarious laughter is heard.

When he is angry, he shouts. And screams. Loudly.

He cannot do that to dad and mum.

So instead? He takes his frustration out on me
And I find that really unfair. Not fun.

We have times when we play together, almost silently,
Him humming to my old favourite, Thomas the Tank Engine.
I think he wants to talk to me, he just does not know how, yet;
Even I know that being rude is not his intention.

I love him, and I always will,
But it is as if the world revolves around him.
Because when he cries, laughs, or gets angry,

He gets all of mum and dad's attention.

I know that this is not true, all of the time.
I am just telling you how it feels

To have a sibling who plays so 'differently',

When, if I am totally honest? It's not an 'ideal'.

If only there was a way

That me and my brother could play in harmony.

Understanding and appreciating each other

And not let 'different' be what is separating.

ROW IN THE UNKNOWN

ROW IN THE UNKNOWN

ASC - Potentially Also Me?

So you have just got your diagnosis;
I am seven, you are three.
You meet all of the criteria, tick all the boxes,
But why are they not considering me?

Yes, you have many struggles
From socialising to playing to living life.

But I think what they don't seem to notice is that
There is definitely a sense of strife.

What I mean when I say that is
That I have difficulties, too.
Yes, they may not be as critical as yours;
But surely what equally matters are my views?

I have no true 'friends',

I can't cope with socialising with many.

I hate loud noises, strange smells, weird textures;

Surely, in terms of criteria, that's plenty?

It definitely does not stop there, though.
The fear of abandonment, change
Is too much for my brain to handle
As I cling onto everything within my range.

I love order in my life.
I abide by every single rule.
But still, you can only see his problems;

And I think that's almost cruel.

Just because I can 'mask' better than him,

Does not mean I don't have my days
Where I wish everything would just stop, at least pause.
I want to leave and never come back - away.

Bra's and Ballet

'To continue attending my class,

You must wear, under your leotard, a bra.'

I did not understand what a 'bra' was';

Is this some kind of 'ballet law'?

I remember going to the shop with my mum
But before this? I was on my knees begging to stay
At home and not grow into what I feared,
Someone who had to live in this way.

I wanted to be like my brother, more than anything.
No top at the beach and shorts in the pool.
But I had to be a girl, slowly becoming a woman,

And, in my diary? It is written 'this is NOT cool!'

But I bought the bra and conformed
For another fourteen years.
It took that long for me to learn
That wearing a bra did not equate to tears.

Little Aoife, I want you to know
That one day, that bra will be gone.
You will never have to wear it again,
And the past? Completely forlorn.

Sleepover Shenanigans

Making a fort under the covers
In the adult's king size bed.
Playing kings and queens and servants,
Until the moment we learned to dread.

'Night, night, folks - time for bed',
My aunt calls, signaling us to our bedroom.
We pretend to sleep, but under our fortress
We continue our game; our imaginations bloom.

I am the Queen, when I always wanted to be King
But I know not to argue, ruin the fun.
It is all pretend anyway, right?
I do not actually want my own kingdom to run?

The little ones sneak in, after their bedtimes
Wanting to join in on the excitement.
However they are banished, servants, not needed,
And then we begin our banquet.

All of our favourite foods piled on to the bed,
As far as our eyes can see.
Party Rings, Midget Gems, Jammy Dodgers;
If only it is as real as our minds run free.

We construct the castle so that it is as tall as the ceiling
And take turns jumping from the top.
But as we tire ourselves out from laughing,
We know that it's time for our fun to stop.

Little Aoife, these were some of the best days of your life,
Moments to hold onto.
Never forget your once best friends
Who helped shape Rowan into who has become 'you'.

Irish Dancing

Three beats together
I have learned, is a 'treble'.
You have to hear every beat
As clear as a bell.

'One, two, three's' are easy enough,

As well as my 'seven's' and 'hops'.
But my asthma keeps getting in the way,
Forcing me to take a break, to stop.

It's not just my asthma that makes me stop,
It's the anxiety, the fear of dancing on stage.
I tell my teacher, and she tells me 'not to worry',
It's because I'm still young, still learning. My age.

I don't really feel as though I 'fit in' with my class.

It's very much like school in that way.
But I am here to dance and learn,

To not let being 'odd' lead me astray.

My favourite dance is the 'Slip Jig',
The one where I feel as light as a fairy.
When I jump, free, with my growing strength,
Nothing seems daunting or scary.

I would really like to make some friends here,

But everyone seems to have a 'group'.

It's something I have been used to all my life

But I definitely feel quite 'out of the loop'.

Irish dancing has become my escape,
And although I am alone in the class,
I focus on the choreography, the rhythm, the technique,

And hope this 'left out' feeling will pass.

Netball vs. Football

Football is for the boys,
Netball is for the girls.
But it feels so much like those days in nursery
Where this? Really gets on my nerves.

All of my life so far,
I have been a girl, growing into a teen.
What if that is not what I want to be?
What if I do not want to be seen?

But I am seen, very clearly,
Because I do not play netball; I play soccer.
Which to most of the boys and girls in my class
Comes as a pretty big 'shocker'.

However, a lesson I have learned the hard way through primary school
Is that I might never 'fit in', not in the way that is expected.
I can do my own thing, though,
And not worry about consequences.

It is one of the reasons I get bullied,
But I don't feel like talking about that now.
All that matters is that, right now, I can be both.
But as I grow up? I am not really sure how.

ROW IN THE UNKNOWN

A Chapter Closed

I have spent the last seven years hiding
In plain sight, but you still are not able to see
Who I am, what I like, who I like;
I guess at this point? I don't know what makes 'Aoife', 'me'.

I have been trying to tell you all since day one
That I do not think I identify with my given sex.
But you told me 'It's just a phase, you'll grow out of it',

Yet here I am, waiting for what's next.

Secondary school is a chance
For me to discover who I truly am.
To embrace Aoife for who she is.
Am I even a 'she'? My head is crammed.

Maybe I will find my people,
People who understand.
I can keep hope alive, for a little longer, I guess.
Maybe find someone who can give me a helping hand.

Well, Aoife, it's Rowan here now,
And unfortunately that hand caused abuse.
But your new chapter is a step closer to becoming 'me',
Or whoever you wish to choose.

CAMHS

'You're so ill, Aoife. Look at yourself,'
As my parents plead and beg
For me to see myself through everyone else's eyes.
I bounce and bounce my right leg.

We are in CAMHS to get me 'help' for the first time.
I don't know what 'help' means.

But apparently the reason for that is because I'm unwell,
Even though, internally, I know I am falling apart at the seams.

The lady who comes in to 'assess' me
Checks everything from height to weight.
When I step on the scales, her face falls into shock;
This is obviously not something she had anticipated.

She asks me questions about how I'm feeling.
I say: lost, alone, sad.
When there is so much more I could open up about
But my mind? Views her as 'bad'.

I was right, she is 'bad', because she wants me to come back,

Every single week until she 'sees improvement,

In my mood, weight, anxiety and stability';

Am I like her newest 'recruitment'?

I get back in the car, and as soon as the doors slam,
I scream abuse at my parents.
'How am I ever going to get better, huh?'
And they look at me like they are the adolescents.

They explain to me that if I want to continue
In life and as the Aoife they know,
I have to cooperate, listen to the lady.
Oh, Mum and Dad, there's so much I wish I could show.

Food and Me

Me and food.
Food and me.
Although it's so important?
I do not see it as a necessity.

I know I am sick.
I know eating will make me well.
But the process of my body changing?
Of everything beginning to swell?

That utterly terrifies me,
To my deep, empty core.
I do not know how to increase calories;
I do not know how to 'eat more'.

My life is calculated by numbers.
I limit my intake every day
To keep those numbers on the scales
As low as possible, so I can one day feel 'okay'.

But although the numbers keep dropping
Through over-exercise and restriction,
I am far from satisfied.
Is this what the lady at CAMHS meant by 'addiction'?

I want to get better, without gaining weight.
But that is impossible, something my parents always say.
So now I spend all meal times at home, alone in my room.
That is the way it needs to be, for now; the way it needs to stay.

Oh, Little Aoife, if only you knew,
That food is one of the best things on this planet.
You will beat this phobia and learn to love yourself,
Although right now it is terrifying. I get it.

Bullying

How can someone, the same size as you
Make you feel so small?
Have that much of an effect on you
That, from everyone, you are withdrawn?

How can people sleep at night
Knowing they have told someone to die?
Someone who has never done anything to them
Who sits alone at night and cries.

How can people threaten to hurt
Your family, those you love most?
Where is the guilt, the remorse, the care
For that person? But no, they just sit and boast.

They boast about how fabulous their lives are
When you know for a fact that they are shit.
They make you feel like gum under their shoes
That is constantly there. To them? You're an 'it'.

Calling someone 'it'
And making everyone else do it too?
How can they live with themselves that you, yes you,
Have crushed that person's dreams, well and true?

Well, Little Aoife, like you said,
Their lives are nothing to be proud of, nor are they.
You just keep being you and fluttering your wings
Because when you're soaring? You won't have them in your way.

Bathroom Dining

When they scrutinise everything you eat and drink
It is so much easier to be alone.
So I came up with a plan in my head of where I can go;
My version of eating by myself at home.

When the bell rings for break and lunch,
I leg it straight to the bathrooms.
I can slip through the crowds fast, not to be seen.
No-one needs to know what I do.

I go into the cubicle, furthest from the door
And start to unpack my lunch.
Everything is wrapped in cling film
So the noise levels? Not that much.

If I am opening a packet of popcorn
And there is someone in the bathrooms, too,
I just call, 'I'm on my period!'
And they apologise and leave me. Phew.

Little Aoife, it's Rowan here
And I just wanted to let you know
That eating in the bathrooms? That's torture.
You should walk into the canteen, and let them know.

Let them know you are the stronger person
Who has nothing nor nowhere to hide.
You deserve to be there, as much as the rest of them.
Don't you dare let them step on your pride.

ROW IN THE UNKNOWN

Beach View

I have not seen the lady in CAMHS
For a long time, since she has not been working.
It is my first appointment after weeks of my parents arguing
To get me seen to, as my health? Is reaching the point of no returning.

The lady takes one look at me
And I have to sit in the waiting room
Whilst she talks and gossips about me to my parents.
Meanwhile, my dark cloud looks like gloom.

I have started seeing and hearing things
That are apparently 'not real', 'not reality'.
I struggle with this concept, because to me?
I cannot always tell what is 'real' and what is 'fantasy'.

I am called back in, my parents almost crying
As I am told I am being hospitalised.
I have to go home and pack a bag immediately.
Where is my say? Is this not my life?

We drive home, pack a bag, drive to the hospital
Which, even though there is no beach, is named 'Beach View'.
I am negotiating with my parents in the car,
'I'll get better this time, I want to'.

But we arrive inside, and the thing that hits me first
Is the overpowering scent of cleaning detergent.
I am rushed to one of the 'meeting rooms',
My parents being told, by staff, my status is 'urgent'.

Rowan here. You'd think I'd have gotten the 'help' then
That I so desperately needed. But instead?
I was turned away. A lost cause. Nothing.
    All to do with the nationwide epidemic: 'no beds'.

School's Out

You would think that leaving school
Would be a celebration of sorts, a party.
But when it is due to you being so unwell,
And at a crucial age - only fourteen?

It is then not so much of a celebration.
There is a hell of a lot of guilt. Shame
That you have let your education slip from under you
And you feel fully as though you are to blame.

You are left with nothing for months
No schedule, no rules, no plan.
You spend your days in bed or on the sofa
Back to where it all began.

You would think in five years you would have made progress
With your mental health and well-being .
But in reality? You are stuck. You are lost.

You do not know what you are even feeling.

Well, Little Aoife, I am here to tell you
To hold on. Fifth year will be better.
You'll go back to school, one day, in your time.
You could always start writing letters?

ROW IN THE UNKNOWN

Homeschooling

Ten o'clock, the doorbell rings.

It's the same every Tuesday.
This is the most out-of-routine day of the week:
I like to call it 'Tutor Day'.

Homeschooling is hard
Considering I am teaching myself half of everything.
But the tutors that I have are helpful for questions
So I do not feel as though I am drowning in anything.

I fly through English,
ICT is a breeze.
I struggle with Maths.
And languages? No, please!

The hardest part, though, is getting out of bed.
Most days my biggest achievement is leaving my room
But now? I have a reason, a purpose, a goal.
I want to get the best grades I can in my 'gloom'.

That's what I call my depression: 'gloom'.

It's a dark cloud constantly lurking.

When I'm trying to concentrate, torrential rain falls on me,

And I can feel the 'gloom' almost smirking.

My exams are soon.
I don't feel a lot.
Anxiety, yes, always.
But the rest? Not a lot.

Little Aoife, you'll end up with grades you did not imagine:

Seven, yes, SEVEN, GCSE's!
How incredible is that, even the ones you self-taught?
You'll get through the next two years with ease.

Darkness Within

I am scared of the dark, but I live in it
All through the day and night.
It terrifies, yet thrills me
When I see the sun setting, less and less light.

Every day my curtains and lights are off
Because I mentally cannot cope with the glare
Of beaming sunshine through the windows
Which feels like a threatening stare.

As much as I love it, it haunts me.
You never know what happens in the shadows.
Who is out there? What are they doing?
Am I in danger? Should I open my windows?

But I cannot. I really can't do it.

It is all in my head, I know.

It is just that the fear of letting the light in
Makes me crave the darkness, even more so.

The thing about darkness, though, is that it gives you
A sense of peace, tranquility, calm
Because you cannot see what haunts you, circling around you.
I have control, which has and always will be my plan.

ROW IN THE UNKNOWN

Sixth Form Results Day

All of the hard work over the last two years?
It all comes down to today.
I am on my laptop, ten minutes before 7.00am
Waiting for my fate. Will I be okay?

I could not have worked any harder under my circumstances
Although mental illness took its toll
On my attendance and having to sit exams separately,
But ultimately? The examiners have control.

It is two minutes until seven
When the screen suddenly flashes.
ICT – 'A'. English Literature – 'B'.
All of my anxiety turns to ashes.

I did it, I achieved both my A-Levels
When I was so poorly, so unwell.
I proved to everyone, but most importantly myself
That I could do it. My pride begins to swell.

It just shows you, Not-So-Little Aoife,
That you had it in you all along.
You got the grades you deserved
And proved that you are so strong.

A-Level Awards Night

I was invited, like everyone else
To the A-Level Awards Night.
It will be hard seeing everyone after a while
But, hopefully, I will be alright.

I am in the car with Mum and Dad
Debating whether or not to go in.
My mum goes inside, to see what the craic is
And my Vice Principal said, 'It's about to begin!'

It takes all my courage to walk into that hall,
But we sit at the very back.
They are going through all of the awards
And I find myself beginning to relax.

The awards for English Literature and ICT are announced
And I am waiting for the 'bright' ones in my class to stir.
However, my name is announced to the crowd!
From then, everything is a blur.

I walk up to the stage, twice, and collect my awards
Overcome with pride and joy.
I cannot believe what I have just achieved;
None of the bullies have this moment of glory to destroy.

See, Aoife? You had it in you all along
To conquer your whole school journey.
Celebrate and allow yourself to be happy,
Because the next part? Well, just get ready…

ROW IN THE UNKNOWN

ASC – Actually Also Me?

I was reading through my report for my assessment
For Autistic Spectrum Condition.
I meet the criteria, I have high-functioning autism,
I no longer feel in 'competition'.

I mentioned earlier in this anthology
That I was envious, almost jealous, of my brother.
But now that I am being accepted and seen for who I am?
Who I always knew I was? My brother is no longer a 'bother'.

My jealousy for his 'special treatment'
Was so apparent that I hated him.
I am being completely honest here, with this
But now? I feel as though I can fully accept him.

When you get a diagnosis yourself,
It gives you a whole new perspective,
On life, both mine and his,
A entirely new introspective.

My brother took things out on me
But that was not his fault.
I hate myself for believing it was, for so long,
But he has always loved me. It has me deep in thought.

I can relate to my brother in so many new ways,
Understand his sensory distress.
Overstimulation can cause havoc, inwards and outwards
And I forgive him for every single thing. I'm ready to now progress.

Isolation

I have been in England getting treatment
For over a year. But right now?
I am the lowest I have ever been. Ever.
I feel as though, if water were to engulf me, I would drown.

I am in isolation in my bedroom
Which has become a prison. A cage.
I feel like an animal being watched at the circus;
I am the entertainment on the main stage.

I did and said things that I will not discuss here;
This is about my life and my personal story.
But after being trapped in a room for over a week?
It is almost like a kind of purgatory.

I have the chance to reflect on what has happened,
Every conversation, every act, every plan
That I was so sure that I wanted to go ahead,
But now? I feel like a full on 'mad man'.

I don't want to spend my life
Alone and scared and locked in.
I want to live a life to remember,
A life, as much as possible, free from sin.

From this day forward, things will change.
I want to show the world who I am.
And although change scares me to my very core?
It's what I need to do. I can.

ROW IN THE UNKNOWN

Honesty

It's Community Meeting every Friday
At around three-thirty in the afternoon.
I have a speech prepared that will be life changing;
A speech that has taken hours to fine-tune.

I am coming out as transgender (well, non-binary first)
To all the staff and my peers.
I expect looks of shock and laughing and staring
As, when I finish, my eyes fill up with tears.

But the complete opposite happens.
I am met with an explosive applause.
This takes my breath away, if I am even still breathing;
I have a look around and take a pause.

Everything goes in slow motion;
The clapping, the approving nods, the smiles.
I feel accepted, validated, at home.
I feel as though, with this energy, I could run for miles.

The noise dies down and I am back to reality,
Still not believing what I have just done.
This is the beginning of my journey as a trans human;
A journey that has only just begun.

Rowan, this is the beginning of your path
To being the honest person you are, deep within.
You hid behind lies for twenty-four years,
But now part of the truth is out? You can live. Begin.

ROW IN THE UNKNOWN

I think the thing about transgender culture
Is the idea that you have 'always known'
That you were born in the wrong body or raised in a different way
Than you would have preferred. But honestly? That's the 'norm'.

Whether you fit under the non-binary spectrum,
Or agender, or gender fluid, or queer,
It doesn't mean you have always had to 'know' that.
It is all part of the journey; don't fear.

Just because you haven't 'always known'
Does not make you one bit less valid.
You can own your sexuality and gender;
This is your song, make it a ballad!

You may feel that you were born in the wrong body
But only fully realise this at twenty-four.
Maybe later, earlier, but that is my experience.
And for me? It opened so many doors.

I had the opportunity, as an adult to explore
So many avenues and terminology.
It's okay to find who you are later in life;
It's all part of human biology.

Online Support Group

I joined my first online video support group
For transgender people like me.
I was not sure what to expect.
Would I be accepted to just 'be'?

I amazed myself instantly
By introducing myself as Row.
I said my pronouns were 'he/they',
And it just felt so 'right', you know?

We talked about each others' experiences
Around a variety of different things.
I participated. These are 'my people',
People I feel connected to with invisible strings.

I have independently found a community
Who value me and see my worth.
If only I felt able and ready to do this sooner,
It's almost like a 'rebirth'.

To anyone out there who is feeling alone
And confused and unsure of what steps to take
On your journey to become transgender?
Well all I have to say is - take it at your own pace.

Everyone's pace is different
And my time has come now.
Yours might be similar or completely different
But be patient with yourself, because that is more than allowed.

Binary

I originally came out as transgender
But labelled myself as 'non-binary'.
However, as time went on, this did not fit.
I wanted a label that, in terms of sex, would define me.

So I thought about this concept a lot.
I knew I did not and could not be a woman.
But if you are not a woman, there is one sex left;
And that sex is to be a man.

Men have terrified me all my life.
Typical 'alpha-males'.
But I realised I did not have to be like them;
This is my ship and I control the sails.

The term 'trans-femme' came to me
Through a group I found online.
I could be a male, however have the opportunity
To express another side, a side that's 'mine'.

I can be a man
And wear makeup and dresses.
This contradicts the 'masculine' stereotypes
But it is my choice how, outwardly, I express.

I know I am a transgender male
But I also know that, now, I can be femme.
So for everyone out there who is confused about boundaries?
Well, you can say 'screw them!'

Loss

I was going to give this poem a miss
Because it will break my heart to write it.
But it could potentially help someone out there,
So I am going to go for it, despite that.

During my stay in this unit,
I have sadly lost two beautiful women, so young.
Two women who had their whole lives ahead of them
But, devastatingly, were taken from them before they had fully begun.

E, we had our chats in the medication lobby.
Sometimes talking rubbish, but the odd time? They were deep,
Meaningful conversations that I will forever hold in my heart.
Conversations and advice that I intend on, for eternity, to keep.

M, we were besties.
'Ginger' and, because of your hair, 'Purple Head'.
We had so many things in common, so many laughs;
There isn't a moment I spent with you that I now dread.

Losing people in the system is part of life
As much as it should not be.
But, as impossible as it sounds, life moves on
And you have to carry on with your own individual journey.

I miss you both so much it hurts
But I hope, if you're looking down, you are proud
Of not only my own purple hair and progress,
But that I am speaking my truths out loud.

If you have lost someone, friends or not,
Hold every positive memory close.
You never know when your last 'goodbye' will be;
So for life and memories in general? Make the most.

'Moo'

It has been three months since I lost you
But it is not getting any easier to cope
Without the person, you, who helped me carry on.
You gave me so much hope.

It is the 'not knowing' that I am struggling with;
Was it on purpose or not?
Did you mean to pass away
Or were you just feeling so lost?

I will be honest with you here.
I have made attempts at my existence.
But every time it was a cry for help.
A cry out that ended up being persistent.

I do not think I ever wanted to die,
I think I was stuck in my 'emotional mind'
Where everything is overwhelming and terrifying
And to myself? I was by no means kind.

But whether it was on purpose or not
It is vital that I continue living for me, and you.
I wish I could share this anthology
With one of the people inspired it, my wee Moo.

ROW IN THE UNKNOWN

Rumination Situations

Tapping, shaking, rocking
Are the 'stims' that affect me the most.
Yes, I do them when over-stimulated, sometimes for pleasure.
However, often? I am conflictingly engrossed.

Most of the time I am not conscious when 'stimming'
Which is a potential difference with OCD and ASC.
Often with obsessional thoughts, I am aware of what I am doing
Because it is to avoid the unthinkable - harm to anyone around me.

I have to do things at certain times
Which is very ASC.
However this need for 'control' takes over my life
To the point where I cannot see clearly.

I could be lying in bed when intrusive thoughts
Slip their way, clandestinely, into my mind.
'If you do not attend planning meeting at this exact time tomorrow?
Your grandparents care? You will no longer find.'

'If you do not eat your food in this exact order,
Every staff member you have a rapport with will leave.'
'If you are not ready to go out at one-thirty on the dot,
To your fellow residents, you will be hatefully perceived.'

To you, and to me reading aloud,
These sound so illogical, with no reason.
But to challenge these thoughts, and not act on them?
My 'emotional mind' sees similarities with treason.

I try every hour to suppress these urges
But the thoughts are stronger than love.
Because when you live like this, every day?
They are seemingly impossible to get rid of.

Letting Go

It can be next to impossible sometimes
To say 'so long' to those you adore.
Especially when they are continuing in life
And you feel as though you are trapped behind a glass door.

You know they miss you, because you miss them
But sometimes? A break is needed.
Time out to refresh and renew the mind
Even though our relationships have receded.

Love is a complicated thing,
But I always say, 'if you love something, set it free.'
For my own personal journey?
This has helped me become… me.

I will always love those close to me,
Hold on to the good times in the past.
But also remembering the bad times, the hardships,
That will, in my head, forever last.

I guess, if you're reading this, I am sorry.
For the anger, upset, loss and pain
That I have caused you, without fully knowing at the time
However that is not an excuse. I am just trying to explain.

However, despite all of the emotional damage,
I have bounced back stronger than ever.
I hate that this may have completely broken you
But I truly hope that, in time, things get better.

Rowan, you have made monumental steps
In your journey to see how 'Row Grows'.
Keep hoping and praying that one day?
Those you love will see that, and contact may be bestowed.

To 'Little Aoife'

I can see you. I can hear you. And I can understand you.

You've been through a lot in your short yet meaningful life. Drama from literally every direction: family issues, so-called friends treating you like you're dirt on the bottom of their knock-off 'designer' shoes, bullying not only in school but at dance, at musical theatre - stealing the things you love right from under you; you've had a lot going on. And I am here to say that just because all of that horrendous trauma happened; your little life is far from over. You may want it to be, right now at this moment in time, but remember this. This is simply just a moment. And moments always pass, like clouds floating calmly on a bright Spring day.

All of your hardships are valid. I know me saying that doesn't make them go away, but I know for a fact that they will make you stronger. To the 'person' you have always dreamed of becoming, leading the life you have always wanted to live. That can happen, and it will happen. All because of that inner strength that flows through you and will surface when you least expect it.

Speaking of life? You have so many things to live for. Your grandparents you love so much? They will become your best friends, your 'partners in crime'. You will see One Direction seven times (yes, seven) live in concert and get to the barricades for nearly every single one. At those concerts, you will make friends for life. True friends this time, not some of the little shits you went to school with. You will meet people like you, people who just 'get it'. People who 'get' you.

So basically, long story short, you have years and years of happiness, excitement, thrills - all of it - ahead of you in a very long, fulfilling life. Yes, there will be ups and downs, some of those downs will nearly break you but like I said before - they will make you stronger.

To conclude, this is a goodbye and a 'hold on to hope' from your future self. You have got this.

Lots of love, Rowan.

To Future Rowan

Hi Row.

So you've published an anthology. How 'cracker' is that?! You've survived so much that a lot of people your age will never go through in a lifetime. But like I said to 'Little Aoife'? These experiences have made you stronger, and I'm sure you realise that.

I want to say 'thank you', so, so much, for being patient with me through all of those difficult years. You never gave up, despite almost doing it several times; but ultimately, you kept going. For the 'Little Aoife' who, to this day, is spurring you on to become a Northern Irish trans icon. Maybe you've even gone down the Drag Queen route. If you have, can I know your name?!

I hope you're living the life you dreamed of, using your chosen pronouns, and have made a family of your own. I hope you have found 'your people' who understand and listen and appreciate every amazing and inspiring thing about you and this hell of a journey you've battled through. It was a battle, but ultimately you won the war.

Rowan you changed my life for the better and I'm so glad I found you within me. Your power, your perseverance, your resilience is nothing short of incredible and I hope you know that.

Please continue being your authentic, true self.

Catch you later.

'Little Row'.

Epigraph

"The bottom line is that if you are in hell, the only way out is to go through a period of sustained misery. Misery is, of course, much better than hell, but it is painful nonetheless. By refusing to accept the misery that it takes to climb out of hell, you end up falling back into hell repeatedly, only to have to start over and over again."

Marsha M. Linehan's, DBT Skills Training Book, 2014

ROW IN THE UNKNOWN

Acknowledgements

I would love to begin by saying a massive 'thank you' to you, yes, YOU, for reading my anthology. This has been a project that I have been working on consistently for over a year and it is a dream come true to have my work published for the public to read.

A big shout-out to my teachers at both primary and secondary school for nurturing my love of poetry. Without you, none of this would have been possible.

Through primary school I had my first poem published through 'Young Writers UK'. It was titled 'Imagine' and was my first published work in an anthology – I find it unbelievable that I have now written my own!

I was lucky enough to meet so many amazing service users through my current unit and past units. From cosmic queens, to 'crazy cat ladies', to fake-tan goddesses, to just genuinely inspiring, top-class humans. All of you who I have grown to love have influenced so much of this anthology in the most positive ways imaginable, and I am beyond grateful to have you all in my life. I wish I could write something for every single one of you but then the acknowledgements would end up being longer than the anthology...

To the staff at my old unit, thank you for being there for me and literally saving my life. You are all not only 'good eggs', but 'excellent eggs'.

That brings me on to staff at my current unit. Each and every one of you have been involved in such a monumental part of my recovery journey and my appreciation for you all will never go unnoticed. To my first DBT nurse, you are the DBT queen and never forget that! To my second? Well... I'm joking! We had our rough patches but I'm so thankful for our little (long) chats towards the end of my stay in the unit. To honour all the work you did with me, I will 'keep making good choices'. To the 'main team' who meet every Monday through to Friday – you have shown me nothing but respect and compassion and that has helped me in my darkest days. Do you know what I mean? Sorry, bear with. And to a certain someone with the initials M.T? You are the inspiration behind so much of this. Words will never convey how much that means. Keep being you, rocking heeled boots higher than the notes your icon hits! I hope you will always remember me for my legendary Nadine Coyle impression.

To my family, whether we are currently close or not so much – thank you. Thank you, thank you, thank you. My love for all of you is unconditional, despite everything that has happened, and please know that you are all forever in my hearts.

To those special people who cannot be here to read my anthology, you will never be forgotten.

Thank you.

ROW IN THE UNKNOWN

Help and Support

Transgender Support:
Spectra
0800 587 8302 / 020 3322 6920
https://spectra-london.org.uk
info@spectra-london.org.uk

Stonewall
0800 0502020
https://www.stonewall.org.uk
https://www.stonewall.org.uk/contact-us

Autistic Spectrum Condition (ASC) Support:
National Autistic Society
0207 833 2299
https://www.autism.org.uk/
nas@nas.org.uk

NHS
https://www.nhs.uk/conditions/autism/support/

Mental Health Support:
Mind
+44-300-123-3393
https://www.mind.org.uk
info@mind.co.uk

Samaritans
116 123
https://www.samaritans.org
jo@samaritans.org

Shout
85258 (Text only)
https://giveusashout.org
info@giveusashout.org

ROW IN THE UNKNOWN

Rowan O'Keefe – Writer Profile

Rowan O'Keefe, (born in 1998 as 'Aoife' (female), however now uses non-feminine pronouns) has always shown a keen interest in creative writing, especially poetry. They had their first poem published in an anthology when they were ten years old which grew their passion for literature.

Throughout school, they flourished in English Literature classes and adored learning the fundamentals of poetry, and how they themselves could improve their writing. They have their wonderful teachers to thank for this.

Rowan struggles to this day with mental health conditions, present in their life since they were nine years old approximately, and are currently in an inpatient unit to aid their recovery. However they are, at present, engaging well in their care programme and have many plans for the future – a life outside hospital. Attending university is a huge part of this, with the intention of, one day, leading a life that is not controlled by poor well-being.

Rowan was also formally diagnosed with ASC (Autistic Spectrum Condition) when they were twenty-four, May 2022, and believe that this has been the 'puzzle piece' that was missing in their life for so long. They don't view neurodivergency as a negative – quite the opposite, in fact. Rowan says it is their 'superpower' which has given them the ability to see the world from a different, interesting and ever-changing perspective.

In July 2022, Rowan 'came out' as transgender to the people in their unit, friends and family. This was a monumental step in Rowan's journey to becoming 'who they were meant to be' and a massive step on the road to further self-discovery, a lifelong process.

Rowan is overall content with their life and cannot wait to see what the next chapter holds. They hope you gained something from reading their anthology – whether that is increased understanding, raised awareness, validation, feeling 'less alone'; perhaps all of the above.

Lightning Source UK Ltd.
Milton Keynes UK
UKHW022032141022
410475UK00015B/775